# PUTKINS.

HEIR TO—

# CASTLES IN THE AIR.

A Comic Drama,

IN ONE ACT.

BY

WILLIAM R. EMERSON.

BOSTON:
GEO. M. BAKER & CO.
Nos. 41-45 Franklin Street.

## CHARACTERS.

John Putkins, *Census-taker.*
Jerry Dolliman.
Phœbe Twist.
Jane Abigail Perkins.

---

## COSTUMES.

Putkins. Black swallow-tail coat, buttoned up tight; broad-brimmed black hat, with deep weed; black Lisle thread gloves; tight black pants; black neck stock, no white showing; spectacles; decidedly seedy throughout.

Jerry. Fustian cut-away coat; red vest; blue necktie, white spots; gray corduroy pants; red stockings; slouched hat.

Phœbe. Picturesque short dress, in bright colors.

Jane. Eccentric old maid's dress.

Time of representation — Forty-five minutes.

---

# PUTKINS.

SCENE. *A Kitchen; a table, containing a pumpkin, tin dishes, big loaf of bread, coffee-pot, &c.; four chairs, broom, dust-pan, &c.*

*Enter* PHŒBE, D. R. C., *with umbrellas.*

*Phœbe.* There wasn't a solitary umbrella in the house last rain, and my poor Jerry not only got wet through coming here, but wet througher going away from here, and all because there wasn't an umbrella to lend him. So this time I've searched the house through, and brought to light no less than thirteen — some blue cotton, and some green cambric; one a sick yellow when it's wet, and no color when it's dry; some with handles, and some with everything but a handle. Dear me; what a wicked world this is, to be sure! There ought to be a new commandment made about umbrellas. I've seen our deacon, coming out of meeting, deliberately contemplate his own and the sexton's umbrella, and decide in favor of the latter; and when Aunt Tildy, that sainted woman, goes out to visit the poor, with a shabby umbrella, she invariably comes home with a better one. If the world ever does burn up, I do believe the fire will start in an umbrella shop. Here's one (*opening an umbrella*) that looks like a balloon they send cats down in; that's good (*kicking another*) to frighten cows with; and this one — this lovely gingham — is big enough to make love under in the summer time, so I'll give it to my dear Dolly, for he's the handsomest young man in the country. How all the village girls do envy me, for they all set their caps for him. Then, he's so bright and funny that everybody begins to titter when he begins to speak; and his head is as full of quotations as a pepper-box of pepper, and when he shakes it at you, you are sure of a sprinkling of Shakspeare, Paul Pry, or some of those great minds; and he carries a play-book in his waistcoat pocket. O (*looking out of window,* L.), here he comes, plodding along just as if there was no shower. I'll throw him his green cambric. No, I'm too late. (*Voice and stamping heard outside.*)

*Enter* JERRY, D. L. C., *with milk-can.*

*Phœbe.* How d'ye do, Dolly?

*Jerry.* Do? Phœbe, squeeze me and see. I bring more water than milk this time, I reckon.

*Phœbe.* Not mixed, I hope.

*Jerry.* Mixed? Do you know what the man in the play says? —

Insinuation is a bitterer pill
Than doctors give to cure or kill.

Mixed, Phœbe? I scorn the *insinuendo!* Mixed? (*Apostrophizing milk-can.*) No! — not unless the cow got wet through. (*Puts milk-can on table.*)

*Phœbe.* Why didn't you borrow an umbrella? 'Twould have been yours, you know.

*Jerry.* I know it would; and that's why I wanted to borrow one of the parson. But he said he hadn't one; and, besides, he was going to use it. That man would send a crate of umbrellas to the Feejee missionaries, but the milk of his human kindness would sour unless it was churned in a big churn with his name on the handle. O Phœbe, I was born with a ready-made umbrella, to shelter me from the showers of a milk-and-water religion.

*Phœbe.* There, then, Dolly, I'll give you this one. (*Gives him an umbrella.*)

*Jerry.* O Phœbe, my heart opens to you like this umbrella. (*Opens umbrella.*)

*Phœbe.* Then I hope you'll never shut it up.

*Jerry.* Why, I should have to take the side of the house down to get it out.

*Phœbe.* No, no! your heart I mean.

*Jerry.* Ah, I see. But 'twould be just as hard to get my heart out of the house when you were in it, Phœbe.

*Phœbe.* O Jerry! (*Sentimentally.*)

*Jerry.* O Phœbe! (*Dramatically.*) By the by, has the census-taking man been here to-day?

*Phœbe.* Well, there was a strange kind of a man here to-day, who almost frightened me out of my senses; but I didn't think he meant to take them. It was a drunk butcher.

*Jerry.* A drunk butcher is an object of terror to young women, certainly; but you misunderstand me — cen*sus*, not sen*ses; sus*, not *ses.*

*Phœbe.* O, no, no such man has been here. Who is he?

*Jerry.* A man who takes account of human stock.

*Phœbe.* Human stock! What's that?

*Jerry.* Men, women, and children — great and small, old and young, male and female, of both sexes.

*Phœbe.* I never heard of such a creature before.

*Jerry.* Well, if you see him once you'll know him a second time, for he's a curious man. I saw him this morning at the Man and Beast tavern. He carries a pile of big books under his arm, and has an ink bottle tied round his neck. He asked everybody's name, and the name of everybody in everybody's family, as far back as anybody could remember anybody. He wants to know what everybody's worth, and is very particular to know where everybody's grandfather was buried, and if there are any long and interesting epitaphs on anybody's family tombstone.

*Phœbe.* O, mercy me! does he count the dead human stock?

*Jerry.* And he asks if there are any registers in anybody's Family Bible; and is very particular to know if there is, or ever has been, anybody in your particular family by the diabolical name of something that sounded like Pumpkins.

*Phœbe.* He won't find any Pumpkins in our Family Bible, I can tell him.

*Jerry.* He's a walking directory; a gazetteer on legs; he's been everywhere, seen everybody, and remembers them all. (*Voice of an old woman heard outside, saying,* PHŒBE, PHŒBE, *there's a queer looking man trying to get into the back gate that's nailed up.*)

*Phœbe.* Then there's no danger of his getting in.

*Voice.* He's crawled under the bars, and is reading the name on the hen-coop.

*Phœbe.* Let him read, there's no secret on it. Do you know, Dolly, that poor Aunt Tildy has got some great secret — and she won't tell me what it is — that is wearing her life out. Sometimes she mutters, poor Tom, poor Tom, and cries as if her heart would break. Why, it was only last night, when there was a lull in the storm, and all was so still and awful that I shuddered for fear, she cried, in a low, sobbing voice, "Dear Tom, dear Tom, where have you — have you — been so long, so long?" Then the wind roared in the chimney, and the rain beat against the windows, and I fell asleep, crying like a child. (*Weeps.*)

*Jerry.* Don't cry, Phœbe; don't. Perhaps if this census man comes here, he can tell us something about poor Tom.

*Phœbe.* Why, Dolly, perhaps he can; and I'll ask him all about every poor Tom he ever heard of.

*Jerry.* And I'll ask him if he ever heard of a play-actor in the illustrious family of the Dollimans; and if he knows anything of a poor Tom, and a tragic Dolliman. It will dry the tears in Aunt Tildy's eyes, and "Dolliman will be himself again." (*Tragically.*)

*Enter* PUTKINS, D. L. C., *with big books under his arm, immense goosequill behind his ear, and inkhorn hung round his neck.*

*Putkins* (*catching latter part of* JERRY'S *speech*). Dolliman, Dolliman; where from?

*Jerry* (*coolly*). Haven't the slightest idea where from, nor where I'm going to.

*Put.* Who lives in this house? Is he at home?

*Phœbe* (*courtesies*). Patience Tildy, widow; and she is at home.

*Put.* Our compliments to Patience Tildy, widow. One of the Queen's Commissioners would confer with her. (*Sits.*)

*Phœbe* (*courtesies again*). Yes, sir. A Queen's Commissioner in our kitchen! Goodness, we'll have a new set of tin ware right off. (*Runs off,* R. 1 E. — PUTKINS *makes notes in book.*)

*Jerry* (*throwing a bag over his shoulder, which nearly hits* PUTKINS). Your pardon, sir, but if you want to count me, here I am; but I'm off in a jiffy, like a sky-rocket. (*Imitating sound of rocket.*)

*Put.* Well, sir, what may I call you?

*Jerry.* You *might* call me what you were a mind to, but 'twouldn't be likely to be my name. No, sir, I pass for Jeremiah Dolliman — your servant — in these parts.

*Put.* Proceed, Mr. Jeremiah, with your age, residence, &c. (*Prepares to write.*)

*Jerry* (*aside*). I'm going into his census-book like a supernumerary in a play-bill. Who knows but that name will shine one of these days as a great Falstaff or Hunchback!

*Put.* Proceed, proceed, Mr. Dollarbill.

*Jerry.* Dollarbill? Excuse me, sir, I'm no Dollarbill, and never had an introduction to the family. Dolliman, sir, without so much as a shilling.

*Put.* Go on, Mr. Dolliman — age, residence, &c.

*Jerry.* Twenty-one and about three weeks; residence next farm, &c. — the only so forth I can think of is Esquire. (*Bell heard.*) That's our cow-bell calling me; good day, sir. By the by, I didn't get your name.

*Put.* Putkins.

*Jerry.* Putkins? Putkins? (*In surprise.*)

*Put.* (*aside*). He's heard of a Putkins. (*Aloud.*) Well, sir, what is there so wonderful in Putkins?

*Jerry.* O, nothing, nothing! Only I've been trying for a long time to find somebody to name our new horse after. (*Exit*, L. 1 E., *tragically*,)

*Put.* (*alone*). Putkins, listen to me. You're a brave fellow, Putkins, and if I could un-Putkins myself, I'd take off my hat to you, undaunted Putkins. Day after day, week after week, year after year, trampling under foot every obstacle that rose between you and the magnificent fortune of an ancestor whose sole heir you are, — for to my knowledge you are, may I not say, the last rose of the summer of the Putkins family. Absalom Putkins was a Crœsus. This Crœsus was my great-grandfather's grandfather. None of the Putkinses have been worth a sixpence since this Crœsus died — which minor item in his biography he locked up in his grave with him. (*Takes up loaf, and nibbles it.*) For twenty-three years and seven months have I been trying to find some clew to this Absalom Crœsus Putkins, and where his money went to. I devoted the major part of fourteen years to graveyards, that I might lay my tardy tribute of affection above his lamented ashes, until it seemed to me all the rest of the world was dead but a graveyard. A cemetery was my Utopia; epitaphs were my victuals and drink. (*Drinks out of milk-can.*) You might have found me in the gray light of morning, hanging over some dim headstone, waiting for the sun to rise and light up the tablet; and at night, feeling out the letters long after the most industrious grave-digger had shouldered his pick and gone home to supper. I dreamed obituaries, and fell asleep over requiescats. A skull and cross-bones had no more terrors for me than a jumping-jack. I could have gone in a hearse to a picnic of skeletons, and danced to Jim Crow in a tomb with the doors shut. I felt as if I had one eye in the next world hunting for the spirit of A. C. Putkins, and the other eye in this, trying to find where his money had gone to. (*Drinks again.*) At length I emerged from the dead, and came to life again, and, as good luck would have it, I obtained the post of census-taker, and for nine years and seven months, off and on, have I been counting men, women, and children. But not yet, not quite yet, has anybody heard anything of the long-lost, the lamented Absalom P. And shall I now, after twenty-three years and seven months of unflinching perseverance, quail before any obstacle? No; I'd climb mountains higher than Popo-catter-pillar, and go down to the bottom of the deepest boiling spring in a leaking diving-bell, if at the top of the one or the bottom of the other I could discover one of the most diminutive of A. P.'s traces. Why falter, when I hold in my very grasp (*taking quill from behind his ear*) the key to the vaults of my Crœsan ancestor. Beg your pardon, Putkins, it's nothing but a goosequill. Falter? No, no; my road is too plain, my purpose too deep. If life is to be a waste, I'll waste it all; but until I can feast my soul with some unmistakable testimony of my beloved Absalom, you'll find John Putkins the same old delver still. (*Tap heard.*) Did somebody tap? In the temporary absence of the young woman, it devolves upon me to let that somebody in. (*Opens door.*)

*Enter* JANE ABIGAIL PERKINS, L., *courtesying very low and comically.*

*Jane.* Is Dame Tildy within, sir? I — I — mean how does she do to-day? I suppose this is Dr. Killmall? (*Aside*). The doctor is a widower.

*Put.* If by Dame Tildy you refer to one Patience Tildy, widow, I am led to suppose she is within. (*Hands her a chair, and both sit.*) I beg you'll excuse my saying that I haven't the most remote idea how she is to-day; and I'm sorry to disappoint you by informing you that I'm not Dr. Killmall. I never heard of but one Killmall, and that bit of information I got from a graveyard in Eggsbury, the only instance I ever met of a P. S. on a gravestone, to the effect that the man buried there was the wrong man, but the right man was much obliged for the flattering terms of the epitaph, and would inform the family that he had had his name pricked in India ink between his upper ribs.

*Jane* (*aside*). What an interesting man. (*Aloud.*) What did his wife say when he came home?

*Put.* I got my information from a tombstone; and no mention whatever was made there of his wife.

*Jane.* Perhaps he had no wife, poor man.

*Put.* Why do you call him poor man? Are we all poor men who have no wives?

*Jane* (*aside*). He insinuates that he has no wife. (*Aloud.*) Unmarried — No. I mean, married women are inclined to say so.

*Put.* What married woman have I the honor of addressing?

*Jane.* Jane Abigail Perkins — unmarried, sir, unmarried.

*Put.* Perkins! Perkins! (*Rising.*) Sure it's not Putkins: same number of letters, and both begin with P. (*Aside.*) I'd give something if that woman was a Putkins.

*Jane.* No, sir, Perkins; Perkins I was christened, and Perkins I expect to die. (*Sighing.*)

*Put.* Could no inducement tempt you to persuade yourself that you are, or might be, a Putkins?

*Jane* (*rising*). (*Aside*). Is it possible that he has offered himself. (*Aloud.*) You really must excuse me, sir, but as our acquaintance has been of — somewhat doubtful length — I — I —

*Put.* (*aside*). The woman is evidently laboring under the idea that I wish to make a Mrs. John Putkins of her.

*Jane* (*continuing*). And as I have only just run over to bring Aunt Tildy a receipt for gruel — I — I — should prefer to take a little time to consider. (*Aside.*) What would the old folks say if I should bring home a dear husband, when I only just ran over with a receipt for gruel?

*Put.* Excuse me, Miss Perkins, but for so many years have I been looking, hoping, *longing*, for a Putkins, that my very first impression on seeing you, and learning that your name began with a P, was to embrace you as I would a Putkins.

*Jane.* It would, under the circumstances, have been but a natural mistake, and easily rectified afterwards.

*Put.* What, embracing you?

*Jane.* O, dear; how hot this kitchen is! I shall faint! (*Fans herself with a dust-pan lying on table, which she drops, and pulls out handkerchief, which she also lets fall, and sinks back in chair.*)

*Put.* (*rushes forward, picks up handkerchief, and fans her*). The kitchen is close, certainly. I'll fling open all the doors and windows.

*Jane.* No matter, no matter; thank you. I'm better now.

*Put.* (*reading name on handkerchief*). Spunkit? Spunkit? Same letters as Putkins! Put 'em in a dice-box, and you'd throw Putkins as often as Kunspit — no, I mean Spunkit. (*Aside.*) There's some deep game here. Who knows but they've tipped the name round to destroy the clew to the property. I'll solve the mystery connected with this woman, if I have to marry her for it. (*Aloud.*) Am I right in reading Spunkit?

*Jane.* Perfectly. Spunkit is the surname of my mother's second and present husband, and a common name where he came from.

*Put.* Ah, indeed. Not a wink o' sleep shall come to these eyes till I have skunked Pumpit — I mean pumped Spunkit.

*Jane.* He may give you a good deal of information, for he was a sexton once, and parish beadle now, and his back garret is filled with pictures of family trees, and weeping willows, and framed certificates, and dirty old marriage and death books.

*Put.* (*aside*). He's my man, if she has to be my woman. (*Aloud.*) Did you ever hear him speak of one Putkins?

*Jane.* No; but it seems to me — (*thinking deeply*) — yes, I'm sure — I can't be mistaken — I've read some such name in an old Family Register we have.

*Put.* (*excitedly*). You have! Miss Perkins, my *dear* Miss Perkins! if my everlasting obligation, and gratitude, and friendship, and love, can have any attractions for you, produce that register.

*Jane* (*aside*). My fate's in that register.

*Put.* (*aside*). My fortune's in that register.

*Jane.* It's yours, (*aside*) or J. A. Perkins dies an old maid.

[*Exit*, L., *tragically.*

*Put.* (*following her to door, and watching her*). What a rare creature that woman is. If there were more like her, with the same self-sacrificing interest in John Putkins, the world would be lonely if he couldn't marry 'em all. Bless her, she's left her umbrella! (*Seizes one of Phœbe's, and runs out,* L.)

*Enter* PHŒBE, R.

*Phœbe.* She can't see you, sir. What, gone! Here's his hat and books. (*Looking out of window.*) There he goes, chasing a woman with all his might. Bless me, he's got my umbrella! There, he has fallen down right into the green cambric! He's so tangled in the whalebones he can't get out. Yes, he's up again. Here he comes.

*Enter* PUTKINS, L., *in a wrecked condition, holding the ruins of the umbrella.*

*Put.* If it hadn't been for these bones (*pointing to umbrella*) these other bones (*pointing to his ribs*) wouldn't have had a sound one among them. How that woman did fly! Her devotion is sublime. (*Seeing* PHŒBE.) Well, dear; what does Aunt Tiddledee say?

*Phœbe.* Tildy, sir, (*angrily;*) T-i-l-d-y! (*spelling it.*) She can't see you. She says she is nothing but a poor forlorn widow; not worth counting.

*Put.* (*grandly*). Young woman! assure your aunt that the census of Great Britain concerns numbers, not conditions; and that widows and old maids are as precious, in the eyes of the true census-taker, as duchesses and dowagers, and, in response to his interrogations, England expects every widow to do her duty. Therefore, in the faithful performance of my office, I would ask your aunt if she ever heard of a Putkins.

*Phœbe* (*aside*). Dear me, I'm getting afraid of this creature. I wish Jerry would come. (*Aloud.*) Yes, sir; I'll run up stairs with your question, and down stairs with her answer. (*Runs off,* R., *repeating,* "*Did you ever hear of a* PUTKINS?")

*Put.* Hour by hour, minute by minute, I feel the reins of hope drawing tighter; and with my two new steeds — the old maid and the beadle, to say nothing of the poor widow overhead — I venture to insinuate that a new impetus is about to be given to my car of fortune.

*Enter* JERRY, D. L. C., *in great haste.*

*Jerry.* Sir, sir, run! The Man and Beast is on fire; and your carpet-bag will get scorched.

*Put.* Yes; but what's my carpet-bag to my life and death registers, and two hat-boxes? What would the Queen say if John Putkins lost his life-books and two hat-boxes. [*Exit,* L., *in a hurry.*

*Jerry* (*watching him*). That man's a study for a — a — what you call — a phreneolologist or a — a —physionogomist. He'd make a good grave-digger in Hamlet. (*Seizing pumpkin on table.*) Whose skull may this be? Yorick's? Alas, poor Yorick! I knew him well, Horatio; a fellow of infinite jest. Here hung the lips I've kissed how oft? Where be your jibes now; your jokes, that set the table on a roar? Get to my lady's chamber, and tell her to this favor must she come at last, if she isn't it already — old pumpkin-head! Imagine this Mr. Census at a fire: Quick, man, quick! the fire is getting in at your chamber window! What do we see? He stops the foreman of the tub, half-way up the blazing stairs, with a "Who's your grandmother?" The undaunted Mose hurls him to the floor with his hose-butt. Springing to his feet, he brandishes a gigantic goosequill in the smoky air, and endangers the life of an old woman hurrying to the door, with a "If you love me, sweet woman, was there ever a Putkins in your family?"

*Enter* PHŒBE, R.

*Phœbe* (*not seeing* JERRY, *and as if in answer to* PUTKINS). She doesn't know, sir. Thinks the name familiar; but would like time to consider.

*Jerry* (*in amazement*). Who wants time, the old woman where the house's a-fire? Pshaw, Phœbe, I made the old woman up.

*Phœbe.* You here, Jerry? You made the old woman up? What are you talking about? I thought that strange man was here.

*Jerry.* No, he's just gone. The Man and Beast is on fire, and he's run for his carpet-bag. But he's left his books.

*Phœbe.* I wonder what they are? (*Taking up book.*) Epitaphs!

*Jerry.* Epitaphs?

*Phœbe* (*frightened, and taking hold of* JERRY). O, Jerry; do you know I'm afraid of that dreadful man, going round in people's houses hunting after dead men.

*Jerry.* Don't be afraid of him. In these arms, Phœbe, you are safe from all the lunatics and dead men that ever escaped from a hospital or a graveyard. But let's read his epitaphs.

John Smith was my name, and I died in my sin,
And I loaf with the unforgiven;
For there never was yet — and they don't mean to begin —
An angel named *John* Smith in heaven.

John Smith was a friend of mine, Phœbe. In fact, he was a good many friends of mine. But I shan't shed a tear — not one. Life isn't long enough, if I once get started —

*Phœbe* (*taking book and reading*), —

Poor Jack, the sweep,
Lies here asleep;
He's swept out his last flue;
He stuck in a stack,
And he couldn't get back,
And his soul flew out of the flue.

Poor little sooty! How the family must have felt that owned the chimney.

*Jerry.* And how the chimney must have smoked. (*Reads*), —

Strangers, pause, and drop a tear,
A menagerie man, alas! lies here.
He gathered hyenas and lions bold,
Like Noah, the menagerie man, of old.

I do declare, those gravestones bound would make a good comic almanac.

*Phœbe* (*reads*), —

> Hid in this dust is the physiognomy
> Of the spouse of Revd. P. Economy.
> True to his name in every particular,
> For a graveyard lot,
> A post-hole he bought,
> And he buried her — perpendicular.

*Jerry*. Buried his wife in a post-hole, perpendicular? That man's soul would have gone through the millionth part of a pinhole without touching.

*Phœbe* (*reads*), —

> Light be the earth on the dust of John,
> And Sally, ditto, on hers!
> Each was the other's paragon;
> And they were a pair o' goners.

How beautiful! What is a paragown, Jerry?

*Jerry*. A perrigown is a — a — no matter now. You may want to know something else by and by, and I'll tell you all at once. (*Putting on air of great wisdom, reads*), —

> Hic jacet, a doctor, who, ere he died,
> Called a consultation of M. D.'s to his side.
> Give me *your* pills — I don't dare take my own.
> They gave: in a wink, he was dead as a stone.

*Phœbe*. I'll throw all of Aunt Tildy's medicine out of the window. (*Seizes a bottle; runs to window.*)

*Jerry*. "Forbear, rash woman, forbear;" save your medicine, and give it to the poor. They dote on bitters as your devoted Jerry does on spruce beer. (*Reading*), —

Here lies an actor who played so many characters that he forgot his own. His parts were principally ghosts; and when he was called upon to give up his own, what a stage fright he must have had, for there was no prompter in the last act; and it was for the benefit of the author. Exit, without knowing where he should appear next.

*Phœbe*. O Jerry, Jerry; you never shall be an actor!

*Jerry*. Yes, Phœbe; I must leave this stupid place. I must have a bigger field.

*Phœbe*. A bigger field? Your farm's so big now you don't know what to do with it.

*Jerry*. Let's both go. You be the lady-love, and I the lover. Listen to me. First night of Jeremiah Dolliman and Phœbe Twist. The house is jammed — pit, boxes, and sky-gallery. Now they laugh; now they cry. They wave their handkerchiefs and throw their bouquets when Jerry, as Claude, pictures to his Pauline Phœbe, "A palace by the Lake of Como, lifting to eternal summer its marble walls; where we would have no friends that were not loafers, — no, I mean lovers, — and read no books that were not tales of pirates, — no, no, I mean tales of love, — while the perfumed light stole from — (*trying to remember the word*) — from all-a-buster lamps, and every air was heavy with the breath of orange groves, and music from — from thick boots — no, no, sweet lutes — that gush forth i' the midst of roses." Dost like the picture, Phœbe?

*Phœbe.* I dost.

*Jerry.* Good. Then Jerry's career as a milkman is at an end, and the curtain will shortly rise on a new act of his life.

*Phœbe.* Yes; and I'll wear a beautiful dress with a satin skirt, and plaid stockings, and flowers in my hair, and corals on my neck; and everybody will be asking where Phœbe Twist came from. Dear me, I shall never think of this old place again. But, Jerry, what will become of poor Aunt Tildy? I never thought of her. Who will take care of her when I am gone, and sit by her side when she's sick, and read to her out of the good book? Who will look out for the hens, and pet the cow, and take care of the dog, and feed the cat? 'Twould break all their hearts if their Phœbe went away and left them. (*Throws her arms round* JERRY'S *neck, and cries hard.*)

*Jerry.* There, there, Phœbe; don't take on so. There's no danger of our going away this evening, nor to-morrow morning.

*Phœbe.* But that was a pretty lake you were going to take me to. Where is it, Jerry?

*Jerry.* Well, really, I can't say. I know more about play-books than geography; but I should guess it was somewhere near the Garden of Eden.

*Phœbe.* The Garden of Eden? Where's that?

*Jerry.* You've got me again. I never was much on Sunday School questions.

*Phœbe.* But if you give up the milk trade, and fail in the acting business, what are you going to do then?

*Jerry.* Fail? Don't talk to me of fail. "In the bright lexicon of youth, there's no such word as fail." (*Tears across the stage tragically, and runs into* PUTKINS, *who enters,* D. L. C. — *Exit* JERRY, L.)

*Put.* (*collecting his breath*). The fire was out before I got there. However, I gathered an item from a fireman that may lead to something. (*Observing* PHŒBE.) Well, miss, what does your aunt say?

*Phœbe.* She says the first known Tildy was a tanner of great property. His partner's name she has forgotten. Thinks it began with P.

*Put.* Began with a P? Celestial initial!

*Phœbe.* No it isn't, sir. C is the initial for celestial.

*Put.* (*abstractedly*). Began with a P? Was my sainted Absalom a tanner? Like a hawk narrowing its circles around its prey, my field of operations is narrowing to tombs and tanneries. If I find him not among the dead, I *shall* among the dyers. Young woman, fly to your aunt, and beseech her, in my name as an officer of the crown, to give me all the facts touching this P the tanner.

*Phœbe.* Yes, sir; and while she is racking her poor old brains about your P, can't you find her something about her T — her poor Tom. [*Exit,* R.

*Put.* Her poor Tom! Tom what, I wonder! The world swarms with poor Tom's. Perhaps it was Tom Tildy. I'll look among my books and see. (*Sits down, and turns over a book.*) D. — G. — T. — Tinkleby — Tildy — why, here's a Tildy, to be sure. (*As he says this, enter* PHŒBE, R., *and* JERRY, L. — *They pause and listen.*) I copied it from an old register: "Thomas Tildy, imprisoned for many years in Spain, on conviction of being a leader in the then late rebellion. Afterwards proved to be innocent. On his release, his family had gone no one knew whither. Indemnified by the Spanish government, he became rich, and settled in Dunwich." (*Hearing this,* PHŒBE *and* JERRY *manifest great delight.*)

*Phœbe.* I'll run and tell Aunt Tildy; but I'm afraid her heart will break with joy. [*Exit* PHŒBE.

*Jerry* (*coming forward*). I guess there's no doubt but you've hit the very poor Tom.

*Put.* I hope so, with all my heart.

*Jerry.* As you know something about everybody, did you ever hear of a Dolliman that was a play-actor? If you have, I shall probably find out where I got my *genus* for acting from.

*Put.* There are my books. Every item I pick up I put down. You can examine for yourself. (JERRY *sits, and looks over books.*)

*Enter* PHŒBE, R.

*Phœbe.* O, sir! she was so delighted that she burst out laughing for joy. Then she fell to crying; and it would have done your heart good to see her. She says you mustn't go away till she can see you; and she'll be well in a day or two.

*Put.* Since it's rainy, and coming on dark, I will spend the night here, certainly.

*Phœbe.* O, that's good; and we'll have supper in no time.

*Jerry* (*aside*). I can't find a solitary Dolliman, actor or no actor. No matter, I'll start the family in the business.

*Phœbe.* Come, Dolly, help me get supper.

*Jerry.* Get supper! (*Aside.*) That's the way. Whenever I begin to feel like Julius Cæsar, somebody's sure to ring my infernal cow-bell, or tell me to help get supper. (*Aloud.*) O, yes, Phœbe, I'm coming. Your Romeo's coming, Juliet.

[*Exeunt* PHŒBE *and* JERRY, R.

*Put.* In the happiness which John Putkins seems to have had the good luck to bring into this poor family, he thinks he sees the Aurora of his own good fortune.

*Enter* JANE ABIGAIL, L., *in great haste, loaded with papers and books.*

*Put.* (*graciously bowing her in*). Ah! Miss Perkins again!

*Jane* (*aside*). I've heard of a Putkins; but I shan't tell him at once. (*Sits. — Aloud.*) I'm sorry I couldn't bring more documents, for our garret is absolutely crammed with them, and it would take you a month to look 'em over. (*Aside.*) O, if he only would spend a month in our garret!

*Put.* Garret full? (*Aside.*) To my tombs and tanneries I now add a garret. (*Sits near her.* — *Aloud.*) And did any of the names you saw begin with a P?

*Jane.* O, yes; there were the (*deliberately*) Pottses, and the Pelters, and the Porridashes, and the — the —

*Put.* (*breaking in*). And the Putkinses, hey? (*Drawing up to her.*) No? So then you can't persuade yourself, under any circumstances, to introduce a Putkins into your family, hey?

*Jane* (*aside*). There's that delicate question again. (*Aloud.*) Well, that depends upon the circumstances. If there were a month's time, and — and — (*Playing with handkerchief, and looking sentimentally at* PUTKINS.)

*Put.* If you can give me any information respecting Absalom Putkins, you'll be perfectly satisfied with the circumstances, I assure you.

*Jane.* O, sir; if this was only in our kitchen, I might talk to you more freely.

*Put.* Kitchen? Tell me of my Absalom, and I'd fly with you to any kitchen, feeling assured that it would be the last kitchen that John Putkins would ever condescend to enter, even if it were a kitchen in a —

*Jerry* (*putting head into door*, D. R. C.). "Palace by the Lake of Como." [*Exit* JERRY.

*Put.* Did you speak, Miss Perkins?

*Jane.* Not a word.

*Put.* Then Putkins's guardian angel must have accidentally spoken out loud.

*Jane* (*aside*). I can delay no longer. (*Aloud.*) Yes, sir, I have heard of a Putkins.

*Put.* Heard of a Putkins? (*Wild with astonishment and delight,* PUTKINS *tears across the room.* — *Aside.*) She's heard of a Putkins. (*Aloud.*) Miss Perkins, I worship the very air you tread upon, the very ground you breathe. How can I repay you? I'll throw my arms around — (*Advances as if to embrace her.* — *Aside.*) No, no; I'll be calm. (*Aloud.*) But where did you get your information from?

*Jane.* From some old family letters.

*Put.* (*aside*). Those letters will make a millionnaire of me. (*Sits near her.*)

*Jane* (*aside*). Those letters will make a Putkins of me. O Abigail, you only ran over with a receipt for gruel, and you stumble upon a receipt for making a husband.

*Put.* Are you confident it was a P-u-t-k-i-n-s? (*Spells it.*)

*Jane.* A genuine P-u-t-k-i-n-s. (*Spells it, and looks over letters.*)

*Put.* (*rising*). I'm calm; perfectly calm. As unmoved as when, in the graveyards of Wales, I came to the alphabetical corner where the P.'s were buried. Calm, yet stirred by a thousand unspeakable emotions; not dizzy, yet standing on a pinnacle that has been building for twenty-three years and seven months. With my eye ever fixed upon this hour, I have mastered a philosophy which disciplines me to bear this announcement with the most sublime composure. In view of this event, which for many years I have expected would happen the next minute, I have prepared a letter

— in fact, have prepared it and worn it out a dozen times a year — resigning my position as census-taker, which, for divers reasons, — one of which was that I got my living out of it, and another that I had not then heard from my long lost Absalom, — has not been sent till now. It is as follows: (*Taking from his pocket a dirty, ragged document, in an immense envelope.*) "I, John Putkins, census-taker, do hereby tender my resignation of such office; and beg that the amount of my salary unpaid be appropriated as the nucleus of a fund for giving a gravestone and a first-class epitaph to every poor defunct census-taker" — a fate from which this angelic being has just saved me. (*Seals it, and calls.*) Jerry! Young man! Here!

*Enter* JERRY, R.

*Jerry.* Yes, sir; here I am.

*Put.* Oblige me by putting that document in the next post. (*Gives him a sixpence.*)

*Jerry.* I'll fly with it. [*Exit* JERRY, D. L. C.

*Jane.* I've found the letter. Here it is. I will read an extract.

*Put.* Miss Perkins, before we proceed further, let me observe that your interest in me and my cause fills me with the most unfeigned admiration; and, in holding out to you the temptation of my hand and — fortune — through your timely instrumentality — I venture to intimate that the transition from Perkins to Putkins is easy and natural.

*Jane.* Mr. Putkins, in ceasing to be a Perkins, I feel the truth of your words: "Easy and natural, easy and natural." (*Aside.*) I shall never forget that gruel.

*Put.* Now, my dear Abigail (*drawing up closely to her*), let's proceed with the letters.

*Jane.* Yes, my dear. What did you say your Christian name was?

*Put.* John.

*Jane.* John, we will. (*Reads.*) "The Putkins you refer to was reported to be immensely rich."

*Put.* The correspondent is correct.

*Jane* (*continuing*). "He is of the family by that name in Sundown —"

*Put.* Is it possible? Sundown was my native place. Go on.

*Jane.* "He was to have been married, but he was absent so many years that the young lady, supposing him dead, married another man — "

*Put.* She little knew what she was losing. Dare say she married a beggar.

*Jane.* "The young woman's name was —"

*Put.* Some countess, I suppose.

*Jane.* No, sir. There it is — Elmira Wilt.

*Put.* (*starting up in blank amazement*). Elmira Wilt? Elmira Wilt? Is it possible! Abigail, the Putkins you have read about is — myself.

*Jane* (*shrieking, and falling back in chair*). O dear! O dear! Rather than to have imposed upon you in this trying manner, your unsuspecting Abigail, in her innocence and loneliness, would willingly have gone to her grave under the Balm o' Gileads — that's where our lot is. As it is, I release you from any further obligation. (*Buries her face in handkerchief.*)

*Put.* Cheer up, Abigail; cheer up, Jane. What's being deceived in a fancied Absalom to having found a genuine Abigail? No, no; my Abigail in hand shall be A No. 1; my Absalom in the bush, A No. 2. By the by, I must get back my letter. (*Runs out*, D. L. C.)

*Jane.* Who would have thought that a little gruel could have made such a revolution. What will the old folks say? Compare me at supper time with what I was at dinner! Ah, me; strange things happen in a strange world between dinner and supper.

*Enter* PUTKINS, D. L. C.

*Put.* I found the young man just in time. (*Puts letter back into pocket.*) Cheer up, I say, Abigail. Two of us can work in this business better than one. I'll leave you to the graveyards, while I devote myself to the tanneries.

*Jane.* As a Perkins, I should have fainted away if left alone in a graveyard. As a Putkins, my honeymoon will be sweet among the tombs.

*Enter* JERRY *and* PHŒBE, R., *bringing in tea things.*

*Phœbe.* We've got the best supper that ever a king ate — tongue, buns, beans, and doughnuts.

*Put.* I never was hungrier in my life, and I've a particular fancy for every article in your bill of fare — especially your doughnuts. I've a weakness for doughnuts that I've brought with me from my youth unimpaired. Abigail, be comforted. No man can be in great distress who can digest a doughnut.

*Jerry.* Then I don't believe anything's the matter with me. (*Sticking fork in doughnut, and waving it.*)

*Jane.* I didn't think to stop to tea. I only ran over with a receipt for gruel. But seeing you have such pleasant company — (*at* PUTKINS.)

*Put.* You will be persuaded, eh? Well, this is indeed an episode in the experience of a census-taker; and, nothing daunted by any temporary disappointment, I — we (*looking at* JANE) shall still push forward for the great unclaimed Putkins inheritance.

*Phœbe.* How do you like your coffee, Mr. Putkins?

*Put.* (*standing — the rest seated*). Potent, my dear, potent. (PHŒBE *gives him coffee, with doughnut in saucer.*) Feeling assured that, with the help of kind friends by the way, we shall shortly solve, in graveyard or garret, the great Putkins mystery that no tannery can *hide.* (*They rattle the dishes noisily.* — PUTKINS *chokes himself with coffee and dougnut.*)

PHŒBE.

JERRY. TABLE. JANE.

PUTKINS.

CURTAIN.

"Books that our Teachers ought to have on hand to SPICE UP with now and then." — ST. LOUIS JOURNAL OF EDUCATION.

---

# GEO. M. BAKER'S
# READING CLUB and HANDY SPEAKER,

BEING

## *Selections in Prose and Poetry,*

SERIOUS, HUMOROUS, PATHETIC, PATRIOTIC, and DRAMATIC. FRESH and ATTRACTIVE PIECES for SCHOOL SPEAKERS and READING CIRCLES.

In the words of the GOSPEL BANNER, —

*'From grave to gay, from lively to severe,'*
*In poetry and prose a judicious mixture here;*
*Beside outlandish dialects, full of words odd and queer,*
*Which stir one's sense of humor as they fall upon the ear,*
*Pleasant to those who read or speak as unto those who hear.*

Published in Parts, each Part containing Fifty Selections. Paper Covers, 15 cents each. Printed on Fine Paper, and Handsomely Bound in Cloth, price, 50 cents each.

---

### READING CLUB NO. 1.

"We have many readers and books that purport to furnish pieces for the use of amateur speakers and juvenile orators. But the great defect in nearly all of them is, that their selections are made from the same series of authors. We are surfeited *ad nauseam* with 'The boy stood on the burning deck,' 'On Linden, when the sun was low,' 'My name is Norval!' or, 'My voice is still for war.' But in this volume, the first of a series, Mr. Baker deviates from the beaten track, and furnishes some fifty selections which have not been published before in any collection of readings. Mr. Baker has himself written many pieces for the amateur stage, and achieved a reputation as a public reader, so that he is eminently qualified by his own experience for the task of teaching others." — *Phil. Age.*

### READING CLUB NO. 2.

"Mr. Baker deserves the thanks of the reading public for his indefatigable endeavors in the field of light and agreeable literature. The selections are made with good taste, and the book will be of great value for its indicated purpose." — *New Haven Courier.*

"In its adaptation to day schools, seminaries, colleges, and home reading, the work will be found very superior in its variety and adaptability of contents." — *Dayton (Ohio) Press.*

### READING CLUB NO. 3.

"This is one of those books that our teachers ought to have at hand to *spice up* with now and then. This is No. 3 of the series, and they are all brim full of short articles, serious, humorous, pathetic, patriotic, and dramatic. Send and get one, and you will be sure to get the rest." — *St. Louis Journal of Education, Jan.* 1876.

"The young elocutionist will find it a convenient pocket companion, and the general reader derive much amusement at odd moments from its perusal." — *Forest and Stream, N. Y., Jan.* 6, 1876.

### READING CLUB NO. 4. (*Just Ready.*)

---

*Sold by all Booksellers, and sent by mail, postpaid, on receipt of price.*

**LEE & SHEPARD, Publishers, Boston.**

www.ingramcontent.com/pod-product-compliance
Lightning Source LLC
LaVergne TN
LVHW020637110826
845149LV00004B/1250

* 9 7 8 1 4 1 8 1 9 1 0 5 4 *